Adventurous Anim;

Introduction

The adventurous animals of Dartmoor would like to welcome you to their home. They invite you to visit Dartmoor and learn about their lives and habitats while having some fun and a bit of exercise. The animals will guide you through each walk and tell you about the place where they live. From the biggest birds to the smallest insects they all have an interesting story to tell and you can join them. They love living on the moor and hope you enjoy your visit but ask you one thing. Please take care of this wild and beautiful environment and save it for the future generations of wildlife and people to enjoy.

In this book, there are ten walks all around the edge of Dartmoor and they all start where you can leave your car behind. They are just long enough to get a bit of exercise and lots of fresh air. They should all take a few hours but you are always welcome to stay longer to play, explore or just stand and stare at Dartmoor, a place full of natural wonder.

This book is aimed at families with children but will probably be interesting to people of any age. The routes are all dog friendly as they will not take you over challenging stiles but please remember that there are ponies grazing and Dartmoor farmers have livestock on the moor so dogs must be well behaved or kept on a lead. This book aims to help you to find interesting and amazing features of the natural world to admire but please make sure you don't disturb the homes of the animals and leave wild plants for the insects.

The adventurous animals that fly, run, swim and creep around Dartmoor would like you to enjoy your walks. Please be aware that Dartmoor weather sometimes plays tricks on you and conditions can change quite quickly sometimes. If you experience a sudden change for the worse with fog, rain or storms arriving, remember you can shorten the route or retrace your steps to get safely back to the beginning. Always remember to look at the forecast and wear appropriate clothing and footwear – it's often wet and muddy out there.

Navigation note: for the best route finding it may help to take a 1:25,000 scale OS map (OL28) or digital mapping with you as well as using the sketch maps and the route notes in this book.

Contents:

Walk 1: Out of Town - Dormice and Ancient Oak Woods
Start: Simmons Park car park, Okehampton SX589947 (toilets available opposite Okehampton Post Office)

Distance: approximately 3km (1 ¾ miles) or 6 ½ km (4 miles)
Time: allow an hour for the shorter route or 2 ½ hours for the longer route but you may wish to stay longer.

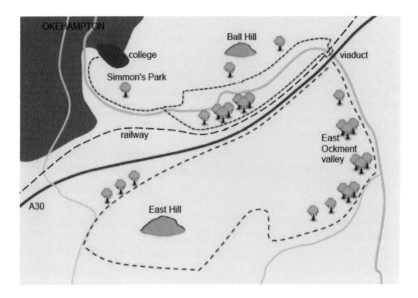

From the car park at Simmons Park follow the East Ockment river along its rocky gorge to the far end of the park where the playgrounds are. Keep following the river through a small wild flower meadow until you reach a small wooden bridge called Pig Bridge where you cross over into a meadow below the woods. Follow the river as it tumbles over rocks. Taking care not to fall in, you can stand really still and look really hard, you may be able to see brown trout. Their camouflage is so good that they look just like the bed of the river but sometimes they flick their bodies to adjust their position and you can see them for a moment. They are waiting for morsels of food to pass by.

Begin to climb the path into Tramlines Wood and look out for some bracket fungus on the way up the hill. This type of fungus lives on decaying wood and, if you bend down and have a close look, you can see the growth rings (like a tree) and work out how old they are.

Though the animals that live in this wood aren't always visible, you are welcome to come and look for them at any time of year. For part of the year dormice live high in the branches and only come out at night; their big black eyes help them to see in the dark. They are a rare and protected animal and woods like this one, with a mix of tall trees shrubs, brambles, ferns and wildflowers are an ideal place to live. During the winter they'll be hibernating in a secret spot under a pile of leaves. In the spring and summer they are busy climbing around, building nests and looking for food to build up their strength.

When you reach the track at the top of the wood, turn left and you will be walking alongside an old hedge bank. Here you will see a whole range of mosses, ferns and wildflowers. The primrose grows here in the spring and is the flower of Devon. Carry on down this old track and try to imagine the tramlines that ran along here over 100 years ago. There is a small quarry at the bottom of the hill and stone used to be transported to Station Road to build some of the houses in the days when the railways were being built. Walking further down the tramlines, have a look through the oak trees and listen for the small birds in the tree tops. One of these birds could be the pied flycatcher. They migrate between Africa and these western oak woods, arriving here in April to spend the summer feeding on the tiny insects that buzz between the trees. There are also some nest boxes here to give them somewhere to rest after their long journey.

Pied flycatcher
by Erin Mortimore

Before you leave the wood you may notice a number of small streams running down the hill. They have created a wet woodland lower down the slope which makes it difficult for people to walk around, but a perfect safe place for roe deer to hide. Pass through the wooden gate and the track takes you out into an open meadow. As you walk down the hill look out for lichen beards in the trees and, as the track bends to the right, the overgrown quarry.

Pass through one more gate and you can stand beneath the Fatherford railway viaduct which was built in the 1870s (**the extended route continues from the wooden gate**).

Though this area is named after the ford the, best way to cross the river is by Charlotte's Bridge. On the other side, a small gate takes you along a lane then immediately left on the Ball Hill path along the other side of the river. This is an interesting woodland as it constantly changes as you walk through it. There's a good mix of habitats in this woodland. First you can see a mixed broadleaf woodland followed by a more open scrubby gorse area. A bit further along you will see some conifers too. All this variety provides the wildlife with some good places to feed and breed through the summer. The dormice are often feeding here during the autumn too, so they can reach a good weight to hibernate. It's a bit sunnier over this side of the valley which they like. I'm sure you appreciate a bit of extra warmth from the sun!

Leave the Ball Hill path by the gate and take the left fork to the bridge over the leat (a water channel that takes water to the old mill building) and make your way back around the edge of the sports field, retracing your steps to Simmons Park.

To take the **extended route** go through the wooden gate, taking you under the concrete A30 flyover. A colony of pipistrelle bats lives in this bridge and, if you are here on a summer evening, you can see them flitting around to catch small flies. If you are lucky you may see daubenton's bats catching flies over the water surface too. Continue to follow the river upstream and keep a look out for otters on the river, though they are very elusive and usually active at dawn and dusk. Again, you are walking through some beautiful oak woodland which, in this part of Devon, hangs on to the side of the moor in the steep river valleys. Take a few minutes to rest or play by the river while keeping an eye open for birds like the tubby brown dipper or even the flashy blue kingfisher. Just before you reach a small footbridge, turn right and follow a small stream uphill through the oak trees. This is a beautiful Atlantic oak wood where the moss on the ground and boulders holds onto a lot of water and keeps the atmosphere very damp. Walk with care on the narrow sections and, where you meet a stubby stone wall, keep right and follow the permissive footpath arrow to the right.

Leaving the oak woods behind you a view appears on the right where you can see Cosdon Hill and Belstone ridge (see the Belstone walk, No.2). Stay close to the fence on the left and keep following the permissive path arrows towards East Hill and, when you see the military camp, walk towards it until you meet the farm track then turn right. (You can walk right over East Hill if you prefer). While you are here, look around for the herd of Galloway cattle with their white belt around the middle. Go through the farm gate and, at the road, turn right down the hill to the sharp bend at Klondyke Corner where there are two gates.

Take the right hand gate and follow the path by the line of beech trees. This stone boundary was built as a "newtake" when areas of Dartmoor were being claimed hundreds of years ago. Continue on this track beside the bracken and scrubby trees. If you are here in the early summer, you will see a fabulous display of bluebells on the open moor. Enjoy the view over Okehampton before you descend beside the A30. The shrubby verge of this dual carriage way has become an excellent dormouse habitat. They are making the most of this long strip of trees and shrubs that connect up their favourite woodlands. Continue down the short steep section of path and back to Fatherford to re-join the shorter route and return to Okehampton.

Dormouse by Maya Oliveira Gubert

Walk 2: Belstone Boulders

Start: Belstone Village Hall car park SX621937

A community café is available at the village hall on Thursdays from 10 to 12 ish and a Post Office is open there on Tuesday and Thursday mornings.

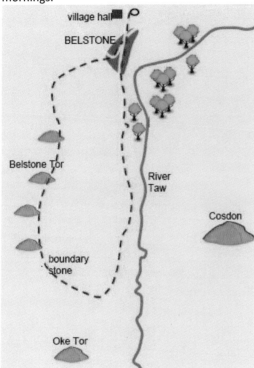

Distance: approximately 7.5 km (4.5 miles)
Time: allow a minimum of 2 hours but there is a lot to explore on the moor and in the village.

From the car park, set off towards the traditional Dartmoor village of Belstone where you can see some great examples of old granite buildings and thatched roofs. Keep walking through the village but look out for Belstone Pound, a stone enclosure where stray animals can be kept until they are claimed by their owners. You may also see a set of stocks which has no longer has an official use but is an excellent opportunity for a photo. Keep left at the green and pass the Old Post Office, keeping left again and along the lane away from the village where a view opens up to the left. Skaigh Valley is beautiful at any time of year and the contrast between the soft woody edge and wide open high moorland is clearly on show here. Continue along the road, down the dip and up again, curving right up to the gate onto the moor. Look out for some vintage farm machinery on the way along the road.

Through the gate, follow the stone track as it snakes along and you emerge into the Taw river valley. As it widens out, the valley is strewn with large boulders. These have been broken away from the granite tors by freeze-thaw action over thousands of years and, on Dartmoor, these rocky areas are known as clitter.

Raven in flight by Laura Parkins

This area is raven country. You might see a pair of large black birds that sometimes perform stunts and acrobatic flight, even when it's really windy. They may look like crows but they are bigger and their distinctively gruff *kronk* call sets them apart. Have a close look at their tail feathers when they fly. The raven's tail is often a diamond rather than a fan shape.

As you keep walking and the valley broadens out you are in Taw Marsh with the backdrop of Oke Tor (the rocky one) and Steeperton Tor (the steep one!). Look really carefully among the rocks for basking lizards on a sunny day, they may stay around to eyeball you before scuttling for cover. Meadow pipits and skylarks provide the tuneful songs and it's fun to try and find these tiny birds high in the sky while they hover and sing.

As the track surface becomes grassy you may notice you are closer to the river. Why not stop and stare into the water to look for small brown trout? Creating dimples in the water surface, you may also see their food, the aquatic insects such as the pond skaters.

Keep going on the grassy track towards Oke Tor but then leave the track and take a small path up the ridge to the right.

Falcons live around here and, if you see a fast bird with pointed wings it could be a peregrine falcon, the fastest hunter in the world. If you are lucky you may also see a smaller falcon, the merlin, which prey on small birds, chasing them over the grassy clumps.

If red flags are flying on the moor, do not enter the zone marked by the red and white poles. This is Okehampton firing range. Instead, where two paths cross, turn right up to Belstone ridge, leaving Oke Tor behind you. Granite tors begin to appear on the skyline in front of you and, once at the top of the ridge, turn right. Catch your breath and stop to look at the expanse of Dartmoor around you. Also notice the marker stones with BB and OPB engraved in them. This is where the parish boundaries of Belstone and Okehampton Hamlets meet. Up here you can imagine you are a raven or a peregrine, spinning, diving or hanging in the breeze. Carry on along the ridge where, half way along, you cross the Irishman's Wall. As the name suggests it was built hundreds of years ago by Irish men; its purpose has always been a bit of a mystery but there must have been a reason for all that hard work. On a clear day the views from here extend right across north Devon to the coast and, sometimes, you can even see Exmoor. Make your way through the boulders while keeping your eye out for more lizards.

Common lizard
by Nathanial Bales

From the final tor on the ridge pick your way carefully down towards the flag pole. Try to avoid using other small paths around the tor. From the flag pole follow the grassy path down to the gate and along the lane back to Belstone. Pass the village stocks one more time on the way to the car park. Adult members of the family may be happy to sit and have rotten fruit thrown at them but do remember who's driving you home.

Walk 3: Cuckoos at Haytor Quarry
Start: Haytor visitor centre car park SX765771 (toilets available)

Distance: approximately 3 ½ km (2 miles)
Time: allow a minimum of 1 hour depending on how far you want to go.

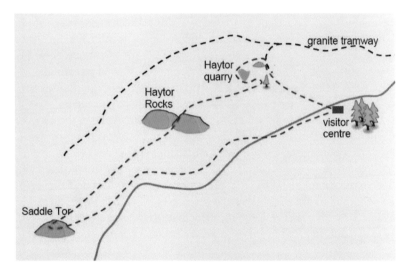

From the visitor centre car park, carefully cross the road and pass between two boulders on the roadside. Follow a grassy track between the bracken and gorse, keeping right towards a rocky spoil heap on the skyline. Don't go to Haytor yet, stand still for a while and listen for the small birds. You may be able to hear many different calls. Some of them may sound similar but others are quite distinct. The sound of two pebbles being clicked together is the call of the stonechat that proudly perches on the top of gorse bushes. Another small bird with a white flash to its rump is the wheatear and Dartmoor is a real stronghold for the species. High above you on a summer day you may hear the endless reeling song of the skylark but there are lots of quieter birds too including linnets, buntings and warblers. This is an important area for many of these birds as they nest in the grassy tussocks and shrubs, and the vegetation is kept in trim by the cattle and ponies that graze here. Keep walking towards the gap in the rock piles where a section of the granite tramway becomes visible. Horse drawn trucks used to run on these stone rails, taking quarried granite all the way to the Stover Canal then on to the coast at Teignmouth to be exported.

Walk round the rock piles on a grassy track, keeping the rocks on your left. It's often quieter here. The habitat has changed and the heather is home to different birds that sit quietly on the ground without perching on shrubs. Where there are shrubs for perching, the cuckoos will wait and watch the ground nesting birds. They are looking for an egg laying opportunity and in the early summer, they will lay a sequence of eggs in the nests of the meadow pipit. Their eggs have become so similar to the egg of the meadow pipit that they often can't be detected in the nest, and when the cuckoo chick hatches it will evict all the other eggs. The cuckoo is famous for its "cuckoo" call and, in the early summer, this is one of the areas of Dartmoor where you are most likely to hear it.

Cuckoo
by Gracie Havard

Keep walking round behind the last pile of boulders and head into the old quarry. Between the banks of heather, a low stile (with a dog gap) leads you into the disused granite quarry. There are lots of wildlife habitats here from the marshy ground to the rocky faces but the most obvious one is the pool where dragonflies will hover and other insects thrive in the water.

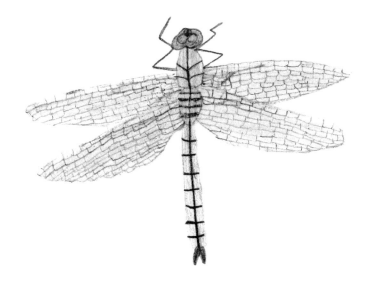

Dragonfly by Gemma Vernon

Follow the gravel path round the pool and through a small gate. Once through the gate look to the right and walk until you see Haytor rock. Climb the hill and explore the rocks where there is a great all-round view. In the autumn you may see flocks of twittering birds swirling around. Wading birds move in from their summer feeding grounds at the coast. You may see them clearly in flight but, when they land, they are invisible!

From the low point between the rock outcrops make your way to Saddle Tor. Avoid the steep slopes and use the well-trodden routes through the gorse. Look down from the high parts of Saddle Tor and beyond the derelict farm and well preserved stone walls in the valley is another popular spot for the cuckoo. Emsworthy is a Devon Wildlife Trust nature reserve. Before you leave Saddle Tor feel the breeze and look out for buzzards gliding on warm air currents.

Find your way back to the car park, only crossing the busy road at a place where you can see clearly.

Walk 4: Water and Temperate Rainforest

Start: Water (near Manaton) SX758806. Turn off the Manaton road along the lane behind the Kestor Inn. There are spaces to park near the t-junction.

Distance: approximately 4 ½ km (3 miles)
Time: allow a minimum of 2 hours and remember, where there is water you may need a good pair of boots.

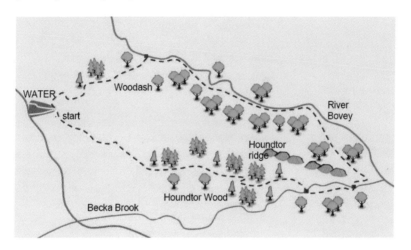

Follow the sign to Lustleigh along the lane past Beckhams. Look at the stone banks of the traditional Devon boundary with the old hedge in the top. There are holes between the stones which are perfect homes for small mammals like bank voles and weasels. Even some birds may nest in them. The bigger holes at the bottom of the wall are rabbit burrows. The old hedgerows are excellent wildlife corridors, allowing many animals to move around and feed in safety.

Enter Houndtor Wood and follow the Byway sign to the left and down the hill. A few veteran oaks stand here but the tall dark conifers are western red cedar and were planted for timber 50 years ago. The Woodland Trust will gradually thin these trees out to allow the remaining oaks to spread and recolonise the woodland. Some of the plantation has been cleared below you and the birch trees and gorse are making their way back, recreating natural woodland.

As the track drops downhill, look along the bank where there is an amazing miniature world of lichen, moss and fern. These species live here because it was once a damp ancient woodland. On the zig-zag bend you can see more tall conifers. These are Douglas fir, planted on an ancient woodland site. This whole hillside will take a long time to restore to wild woodland. You can hear the Becka Brook from here and, as you approach, you can see some large old oak trees along the river side. These trees are used as roosts by a colony of rare barbastelle bats which feed on moths along this valley. Take a deep breath and smell the resin of the fir trees before you leave this area by the old stone bridge over Becka Brook.

Carry on along the track and you will notice a sudden change in the woodland to an ancient oak wood on the steep slopes. This is a very special habitat found in western parts of the UK; Atlantic oak woodlands are so damp they are sometimes known as temperate rainforests. Look at the ground. The rocky acidic soil is covered with mosses and ferns and bits of lichen drop from the trees. The pied flycatcher flies here from Africa every year to spend the summer catching flies and raising a family. Natural England manages this part of the East Dartmoor National Nature Reserve and you may even see their ponies grazing in the woods. Maybe one day Houndtor Wood will look like this.

Pied flycatcher by Jessica Ilott

Take the wooden bridge back across the Becka Brook and follow the path to the end of Houndtor ridge. Turn left and follow and old stone wall along the other side of the ridge. You may find many pieces of lichen below the trees, a sign of clean air. There are some rare lichen species here, making this valley a Site of Special Scientific Interest and it's good to know that the air here is some of the purest in the country. Keep walking and you will see the river Bovey. Listen carefully as you may hear and see otters here. Again, you are in an ancient woodland and, though the soil on the ridge on the left is thin, this mossy habitat acts like a sponge and, as it releases water slowly into the river it prevents flooding downstream.

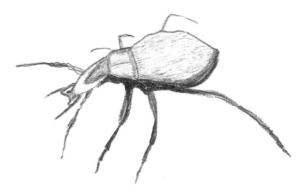

Blue ground beetle by Erin Pengelly
A rare inhabitant but its favourite food is a slug!

Passing through the gate and more temperate rainforest, keep listening for the river as it gets louder. You will pass a boulder jam where the water cascades wildly over the granite boulders. Continue weaving through the woods until you meet another wooden bridge. Leave the river Bovey at this point and climb up to the left towards Manaton, following the mossy stone wall. Pass between the old stone gateposts and follow the signs back to Water. Enjoy your last few minutes in the rainforest before you leave the nature reserve along a walled lane. Keep right, then straight on at a cross road back to Water.

Walk 5: In and Out of the Dart Valley

Start: Newbridge car park SX711708. A public toilet is available in the car park

Distance: approximately 4km (2 ½ miles)
Time: allow a minimum of 2 ½ hours but you may want to stay for a riverside picnic at Deeper Marsh.

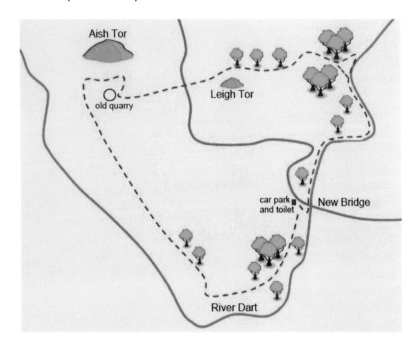

This walk starts in an interesting place, passing under the arch of the medieval stone bridge from the south side then following the river Dart downstream. Looking down into the river, you may not be able to see them but there may be brown trout, sea trout and salmon. Only the brown trout is resident all year round; their life cycle doesn't require them to migrate great distances as do the salmon and sea trout. Keep following the riverside path and the Two Moors Way "MW" signs through the trees and out onto an open meadow at Deeper Marsh. The famous river Dart sweeps round a bend here, with steep rocks and ancient oak woodland on the other side. Look for old, shrubby, lichen covered trees as you follow the grassy river bank. Meet the road at a gap in a stone wall where there are two options:

1 – an off-road route with slightly wetter ground starts directly across the road and climbs into the woods where you find a fence and turn left onto the main route.

2 – carefully walk along the road next to some old iron railings for 100m then cross to a line of boulders where the path follows a fence up hill.

Continue to walk up hill, looking out for squirrels and woodland birds. You may also see ponies as you emerge out onto the bracken, gorse and bramble clad heath. Follow the hazel hedge on your right. Old hedge banks like this are ideal places for voles to hide between the stones and many small birds use them as cover to hide from predators. Keep climbing past Leigh Tor and, if you need to take a breath, take a break to look at the view of the Dart valley below. Continue to follow the hedge and carefully cross the road and walk on the grass between the bracken. You are on the lower slopes of Aish Tor which is a well-known favourite site for butterflies. The sunny south-facing aspect and patchwork of grazed areas, bracken, gorse and shrubs makes it a perfect home for some rare species too. Cross another lane and walk along a stone track towards a disused quarry. When you reach the quarry look on the right for an oak tree where you take the narrow path uphill until you reach a track. Turn left and gently climb on this track until it starts to curve to the right. **(Navigation note)** Take care here to look for a small path that goes downhill through the gorse. Follow the path downhill and stop to smell the bright yellow gorse flowers. Do they remind you of anything?

Pearl bordered fritillary by Martha Pedley

Walking further down through the bracken and gorse you begin to enter a butterfly monitoring site where some of the UK's scarcer species live. There may be ponies grazing on the side of Aish Tor and they play an important role in the conservation of butterflies. The fritillary butterflies, including the pearl-bordered fritillary and the high brown fritillary, need a thatch of bracken to shelter in but feed on wildflowers such as the violet. The grazing ponies provide exactly this habitat and this is one reason why the ponies are such an important part of Dartmoor life. You will also notice that the trees and shrubs are trying to grow on the open heath. The ponies will graze the young shoots and prevent to woodland spreading right across the heath.

Continue until the path meets the boundary, then follow the wire fence on your left. Once at the bottom of the hill you can hear the river again. You meet a track and turn left through the scrubby area. Some of the shrubs here are buckthorn which is the favoured food plant of the brimstone butterfly. This is a large butterfly which can be a very bright yellow – a spectacular sight on a sunny day.

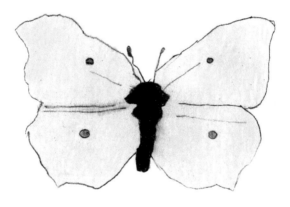

Brimstone by Kathryn Ilott

Stay on the track through the woods and follow a beautifully built wall made of rounded boulders. Enjoy the birdsong in the trees and the carpet of wildflowers before you meet the lane. Turn right and walk back to the car park.

Walk 6: Woods of all Ages
Start: A free car park next to the railway in South Brent SX698602
Distance: 5-6 km (or 3km for an interesting loop round Penstave Copse)

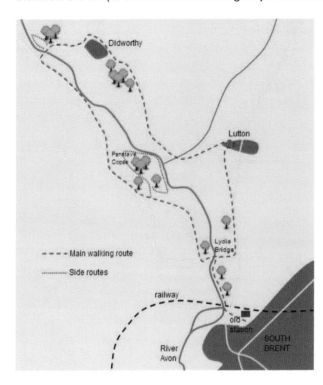

Time: 3 hours should be allowed for the full walk but it can be cut down to an hour if you just visit Penstave Copse.

You could spend all day exploring if you like.

Turn right out of the car park along the old station yard. At the junction, cross the road where a track near the church takes you down to the river. This is the river Avon, a typical Dartmoor river where dippers and grey wagtails fly and brown trout swim, all looking for their favourite tasty insects. Pass a group of tall horse chestnut trees but look out for squirrels dropping conkers. You will soon see the attractive stone arch of Lydia Bridge. Climb the stone steps (admiring the quartz crystals in the granite) and cross the river. Take a moment to watch the water tumbling through its rocky gully. Walk round the bend in the road then find a small stile on your right. Dogs have the choice to go over or under. Follow the narrow path between two stone walls – mind your elbows! After two more stiles, cross a small field and take the stile on the left. This small path goes through a gap in a hedge and into a woodland. This is Penstave Copse and the Woodland Trust have planted trees here after they bought the site in 1993. Woodland creation schemes like this are a long term vision to reinstate wild woodlands and this is a typical example as many of the planted trees are evenly spaced and of a similar size. The species mixture includes ash, oak, hazel, rowan and others that will fit the local landscape perfectly. It is already showing signs of becoming established and the small birds and mammals are moving in. Take the main (lower) path into the plantation. When you reach the next gap in a hedge you have three options:

1 – turn sharp left and follow the boundary up to the lane.

2 – follow the middle track for the main walk along the Avon valley, finding the road gate at the far corner of the copse.

3 – the lower path will take you to the rest of the copse where you can have a look at the meadows and trees, or stay for longer and explore. Sit on one of the benches and enjoy the view. If you decide to go to the old woods down by the river be careful as it requires a little bit of a scramble over rocks.

The meadows are managed for wildflowers and butterflies and you may be lucky enough to see a butterfly orchid here. The old wood at the bottom of the hill is an example of ancient wild wood and, in time, the planted areas will look like this.

The main route continues from the gate at the top of the site (see option 2) and takes you along the lane. A few cars use this lane so walk carefully along here and admire the roadside hedgerow. Hedges are really important corridors for wildlife and, during the spring and summer are full of life. Birds build nests, mice scurry around and bats and butterflies follow the hedge line. Look out for the gatekeeper, a typical hedgerow butterfly. You may also see a large bird of prey flying high. Buzzards nest in this area. Listen for their "mew" call and watch them gliding on the currents of air.

Buzzard soaring by Layne McInnes

When you arrive at the next road junction you may see another small field planted with trees. This was planted more recently than Penstave Copse. Turn right towards Didworthy and cross the river bridge. If you have time for a little spur route, go through the gap next to the gate on the left and have a look at this fascinating little wood. This is private land but the owners have kindly allowed people (and dogs) to walk around. Please read any signs carefully and treat this beautiful little woodland with great respect. Invasive rhododendron is a problem in this valley and the owners are removing it to conserve the wild species here. Clearing this dark, shading plant leaves piles of logs that make excellent places for mice, insects, frogs and birds to shelter and nest.

Back at the road, climb up towards Didworthy house then follow the bridleway on the right to Lutton. Pass the houses and follow the path that takes you past Overbrent Wood. A lot of the trees here are spaced out and of a similar size but not because they have just been planted. For hundreds of years, ancient woodlands like this have been a source of woodfuel and charcoal. The trees were cut at regular intervals and have grown back to roughly the same size. It is now a fabulous habitat for bluebells, birds and insects but, look up at the beard lichen on the old branches. These can only grow where the air is pure.

Kestrel by
Shea Rogers

When you leave the woods, South Brent comes into view again. The farm track you are on has been used for centuries and probably hasn't changed much in all that time. Keep a look out for the buzzards again while you walk down to the ford then climb up towards the buildings at Lutton. Turn right between the buildings and look for a small gate and path beside a field. Look across the valley to Penstave Copse where you can see the meadows surrounded by the planted trees.

Climb another stile onto the lane and turn right down the hill. At the Oak Hill sign at the bottom of the hill, turn right and walk back to Lydia Bridge. Go back down the steps and follow the river back to South Brent.

Walk 7: Out of Town – Longtimber Woods

Start: The walk starts at Ivybridge where Station Road goes under the viaduct (SX635569). You can walk there from the town centre following Erme Road, or park carefully on the roadside near the viaduct.

Distance: 3km loop in the woods with options to extend the walk

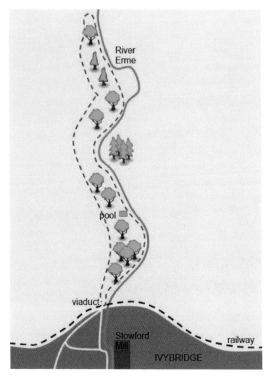

Time:
1 ½ hours should be long enough for the walk but you can extend the walk to and from the town or spend extra time exploring the woods.

Leaving the road, you pass under the viaduct and enter the woods where there is a gradual transition from townscape to wooded valley. A few escapee plants from gardens (Himalayan honeysuckle, buddleia) stand around you before you arrive in a magnificent semi natural woodland with giant oaks and towering beech trees reaching as high as the viaduct. The habitat becomes more ancient and wild as you walk. Look for the mosses, ferns and wildflowers and feel the moist air. There are many clues to the history of this wood and you will soon find the stone walls of a number of enclosures (pounds) which were used generations ago by farmers who were keeping their livestock safe. One was converted into a swimming pool during the second world war.

As you walk, look across the river at the "long timber" standing there. Many of these are north American species of trees such as western red cedar and sequoia and, in 60 years, have grown taller than the ancient hardwoods on your side. Carry on past the picnic area and look up the wooded slopes. The woodrush and ferns give this area a primeval feel. As you walk on you will notice how the tree cover changes to a conifer plantation. These Douglas fir and spruce were planted here for timber and will gradually be removed by local conservationists to allow the ancient oak woods to recolonise the area. The natural woodland edge still thrives here though, and a range of invertebrates live here including butterflies, dragonflies and moths.

Dragonfly by Millie Wilson

With this variety of habitats, you may want to walk here early in the morning and listen to the dawn chorus.

Further along the valley the river is calmer and otters may hunt here – but they will stay well away from dogs and noisy people. It's worth listening for their squeaking call, just in case.

Where a wooden stile crosses the wall, stop and turn left up the hill for the higher route back. (If you don't like the look of the steps you can retrace your steps back).

Wood mouse by Phoebe Findlay Thayre

Now on the higher path, have a close look at the holes in the bases of the mighty oaks and beech trees. This is where the bank voles and wood mice shelter. They sometimes feed in these protected places and traces of nibbled acorns and nuts may be found. Stay on the top path and follow the mossy stone wall. There are more places for small mammals to hide between the rocks. Some of the woodland ground is very wet here and the diversity of wildflowers, mosses, ferns and lichens is a sign of an undisturbed woodland where the miniature world of nature has a stronghold. This is an essential part of a healthy woodland ecosystem. At the end of the wall you meet the lane which you can follow back to the start or, to extend your adventure, drop back down the track on the left. You will see the picnic area again and can return to the start from here. Before leaving the woods, make sure you stand beneath the viaduct and look up, it's very impressive.

Lots more information on this route and other local walks can be found in a very well researched pack of leaflets in the library at the Watermark Centre in Ivybridge.

Walk 8: Waterways and Wide-angle Views

Start: South West Lakes Trust Discovery Centre car park SX552685 (toilets available in the grounds of Burrator Lodge). If the car park is full or closed the walk can start from the quarry car park at SX549676
Distance: approximately 7 ½ km (4 ½ miles)

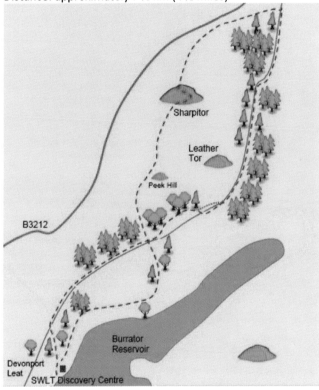

Time: allow 3 hours but you can stay in the area and explore all day.

From the SWLT Discovery Centre car park turn right then take the smaller lane left up the hill. If you hear a commotion in the tall trees beside you it might be the mighty ravens in their nest. They are a large Dartmoor bird and a pair will often return to the same nesting site year after year. At the small bridge over the water channel turn right and follow the path alongside the water course. This channel is called a "leat" and there are many of them all over Dartmoor. This is one of the biggest and the best and was built in the 1790s to take fresh water to the docks at Devonport, Plymouth. It now only flows to Burrator reservoir which became the replacement water supply to Plymouth in the 1890s.

Enjoy the first views along the route as you walk. You can also stop and count the tree rings of the felled conifer stumps. Some of these timber trees were over 70 years old when cut down and, if you look into the deer-fenced enclosure below you can see the planted broadleaved trees that will grow into a natural woodland in years to come. Carry on along the leat and carefully cross the lane to the forest on the other side. These tall trees are western hemlock from North America, planted as a timber crop. Crush a few of their soft needles in your fingers and sniff. Citrus fruit? The next group of trees are sitka spruce with much harder, sharper needles. They are sometime used as Christmas trees and the needles can get stuck into your socks!

Walk through the gate into the ancient oak trees standing among large boulders. Some of the slow growing trees are very old and others have died but are still an essential part of this ecosystem for roosting bats, insects and fungi. They are also beautiful in their own timeworn way. After crossing an area of open ground you see the road and leat but stay on the grass to explore the old stone walls and enclosures.
A gate takes you back into a woodland that was planted with British broadleaves some years ago but, as a reminder, some spruce trees have popped up to show it used to be "Croft's plantation". Wild flowers such as wood sorrel and violets show the ancient woodland soil is coming back to life as the conifers are going. Meeting the lane, turn left and join a gravel track for a short way. There are often ponies around here. Talk quietly to them but don't try to feed them as they are not tame. Once you have passed the ancient burial cairn you cross the leat and carry on along the path to the right of the channel below the prominent rocks of Leather Tor. Walking through the next group of trees you may be able to find needles on the ground that have grown together in pairs. Look up at the orange coloured stems of the trees. These are Scot's pine.

Where the flow of the leat slows down have a look into the water where there are fresh green aquatic plants. In this sparkling clear water you can often see small brown trout darting around, catching a little snack. Keep following the leat all the way through the last stand of conifers and out onto the open moor. Turn left across the leat and follow the old track beside the conifers. Appearing on the ridge to the left are the boulder topped Leather Tor and Sharpitor. Before you get to the road make your way through the pony grazed gorse bushes to the top of Sharpitor. You may be following a line of stones, an ancient boundary.

Climbing to the top of the rocks you are at the high point of the walk and the sweeping view of the reservoir with the soft, tree lined shore and bleak moorland backdrop are worth the effort.

While you are now looking down on Leather Tor stay and listen to the moorland birds like the wheatear and the skylark who sing all summer long.

Skylark by Seth Ramsey

Now follow the grassy path through the bracken to Peek Hill. This is one of the most expansive views of Burrator and possibly one of the best views of Dartmoor. There is an ancient burial cairn to look at here too. From the top, head down in the direction of the reservoir dam to a smaller rock outcrop where the grass path takes you along the contour to a small plateau and in the direction of the deep green conifers. The path descends and you follow the mossy old stone wall and gradually re-enter the ancient, stunted oak woodland. You may hear cackling magpies or chuckling green woodpeckers here. Cross the leat again and walk down to Lower Lowery where you can admire the historic stonework of the barn that was last used before the valley was flooded.

Follow the old farm track down to the road as you look at the deciduous woodland and walls reappearing where the conifers are slowly cleared. Where possible, keep to the grass verge along the road on your return to the Discovery Centre. As an alternative to this final section along the road you can use the SWLT path beside the reservoir.

Brimstone by Chloe Funnell

Walk 9: Haring around White Tor
Start: small quarry car park near Peter Tavy at SX521778 (no toilets).
Avoid using the road side as a car park
Distance: approx. 5km (3 miles)
Time: allow around 2 hours or longer if you want to stay and explore

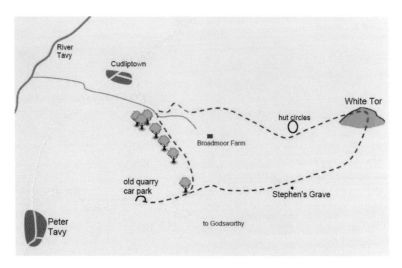

Leave the car park and walk up the road for a short way before joining the track sign posted to Stephen's Grave and White Tor. While you walk look around the sky for birds. The raven is one of the bigger Dartmoor birds and loves to fly around this part of the moor. They look like a crow but are bigger and have a distinctively deep "kronk" call. They are also expert flyers and, if you stand and watch them for a while, you might see a fabulous aerobatic display as they tuck in their wings and tumble through the sky. Sometimes ravens will have a bit of an argument with crows, making quite a noise, but hunting quietly nearby you may see the kestrel, another aviation expert that can hover with precision before dropping from the sky to catch a vole or a mouse.

Hunting kestrel
by Reuben Oliver

Carry on walking where the stone walls funnel you along the track. Look closely at the old stones in the wall. On a hot day you may see a common lizard or other basking creatures but at any time of year you can find many different types of lichen. Examining them closely takes you into a whole world in miniature. Each species of lichen may have a different colour, shade or texture to those next to it and they are all battling for survival to spread across their own piece of rock. How many different types of lichen can you find on one rock?

Once out on the open moor, look to the field boundaries to the left. Just beyond them is a circular feature on the ground. This is the remains of a Bronze Age enclosure which you might be able to explore later on. It was built to enclose a few dwellings and protect people and livestock. Wolves may have been a threat back then but no longer exist on Dartmoor. Another amazing animal that is occasionally seen in this wide open space is the brown hare. One of nature's real athletes, the hare can run fast and, if you are lucky enough to see one, you will be amazed how quickly they move. The hare is secretive and, unlike the rabbit, it lives in a nest known as a form and spends all it's time above ground. In this area of Dartmoor the hare is associated with ancient folklore and the tin mining industry. The symbol of the tinners shows three hares running in a circle with their ears joining together – you may see this in local churches, pubs or in books.

Brown hare by Jack Simmons

There is so much space here and you can carry on walking along the track or run like a hare across the moor but look out for a small standing stone on a triangular plinth. There are different versions of the story but a local boy from Peter Tavy was buried here hundreds of years ago and this is Stephen's grave, engraved with a capital "S". Leaving Stephen's Grave, follow the grass track as it forks left towards White Tor. As the track climbs it crosses an ancient boundary which is linked to the settlement at the top of the tor.

At the top of White Tor there are a number of ancient stone burial chambers to explore and some remains of the Iron Age hillfort that was built in the Neolithic age. Small birds enjoy this part of the moor and you may see some individuals or even large flocks of them. But where do they disappear to? Many of them are ground nesting birds such as the meadow pipit and are masters of camouflage. The skylark is one of the icons of this moor even though it can be hard to see, its continuous reeling song accompanies your walk and seems to carry on all day.

When you have finished exploring the tor make your way down to the enclosures seen earlier. The lower oval enclosure is still very visible after thousands of years and the group of hut circles can be seen on the ground, along with a spring that would have provided fresh water. Turn right below the enclosure and the stone walls will funnel you along a track. Continue to walk by the wall and enjoy the view of Brentor church in the distance. Small burrowing mammals such as the bank vole or common lizards may be seen on a warm day as you walk along the walled track. Can you see small burrows between the stones?
Follow the track and the twisty road until you hear the tumbling stream. A small stone bridge takes you up another track and past a row of tall beech trees on top of a stone wall. Two hundred years ago these boundaries were used to mark the edge of a farm and are still a distinctive part of the Dartmoor landscape today. Continue along the track, through two gates and back to the car park. On the way you might see the derelict and abandoned farm called Twist. Judging by the collapsed roof, nobody has lived here for many years. Life must be tough here for people and it can be a matter of survival for the wildlife too.

Walk 10: Water and Steam, Hard Rock and Ice
Start: Meldon reservoir car park SX561917 (toilets available)

Distance: approximately 6km (3 ¾ miles)
Time: allow a minimum of 2 ½ hours depending on how much exploring you do.

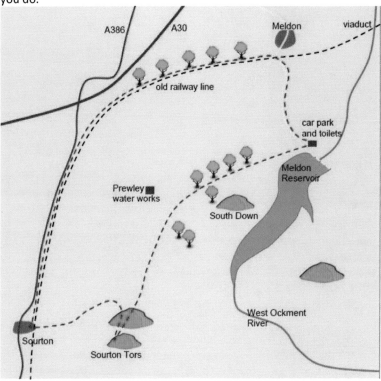

Leave the carpark by the set of steps, cross the lane and walk through the gate. As you climb the grassy meadow Meldon Reservoir comes into view. It was built in 1972 to supply water to surrounding towns.
Keep following the wall on your right where the beech trees stand. These trees are probably older than they look as they have grown slowly since they were planted in the 18th or 19th centuries. Look out for ravens sweeping around these windswept hills. You can tell them apart from crows as they are a bit bigger and have a rougher call or "kronk". You may also see broad winged buzzards searching for food here and even the ultimate flyer, the peregrine falcon nests around here.

Perching raven
by Orson Rivett

Walk between some stunted hawthorn bushes and find a gate that leads you into an old walled track. On the skyline ahead of you are Sourton Tors. Continue on this track and Dartmoor's highest tors appear on your left. An optical illusion makes Yes Tor appear to be higher but High Willhays in the middle of the ridge is the highest by only 2 metres. Once out on the open moor follow the grassy path between the bracken going up to Sourton Tors. Ponies often graze here, creating a typical Dartmoor scene, but don't disturb them as they are not tame. As you walk look out for a set of ridges on the ground below the tor. Explore the humps and bumps for a while and try to work out what they are. They are very unusual and are the remnants of an ice factory built by an enterprising man called James Henderson in the 1870s. This was the time the railways were being built around the moor and the ice was intended for preserving fresh food from Devon as it was transported by rail for sale in the big cities. Sadly, this great idea didn't last long and, hampered by mild winters, the ice factory was soon closed down. Can you find the spring that fed it with fresh water?

Carry on to the top of the tor where a close examination of the rock reveals something interesting. Dartmoor is famous for being a huge chunk of granite but here the rocks are hornfels, very hard metamorphic rock that was altered by the huge molten mass of granite as it rose to the surface millions of years ago. If you look closely at the rocks their flat faces and angular cracks make this part of Dartmoor a bit different. You can also find some quartz intrusions from the molten rock that changed the original sedimentary rock.

At the concrete trig point look down to the church tower at Sourton. Walk carefully down through the gaps in the bracken and head towards the tower – which is actually made from granite! The best route is the old track from the ice factory. Before you leave the moor have a look at the stone walls where many different species of lichen grow. See if you can find crustose (crusty), foliose (leafy) and fruiticose (fruiting branch) lichens on the same area of wall?

When you reach an old bridge you are crossing the old Plymouth to London line which closed in 1968 after less than a century of use. This is now a cycle way but you can imagine the steam trains racing along the edge of Dartmoor. Join the old railway and get some steam up along the old track but look out for cyclists as you pass through cuttings and over embankments. You will pass the Kingfisher pond where you may be able to see frog spawn, tadpoles or frogs. On a sunny day a sparkling dragonfly or damselfly may be seen hovering over the water.

Dragonfly
by Anna Coulson

Carry on walking and carefully cross the lane at Prewley Moor. Looking up to the right you can see the waterworks that treat the water from Meldon reservoir before it is piped to people's homes. Once you are back on the track you can search for butterflies and birds. They enjoy the shrubs and verges and sometimes you can count many different species on your way back to Meldon. Just after the picnic benches you can find a sign telling you how many miles it is to London Waterloo then you leave the old railway at the wooden gate. Walk carefully along the lane to the reservoir car park but you don't have to leave Meldon just yet. Exploring the viaduct and the dam can be great fun and there are some unmissable views around the valley.

RavenQuest

Adventurous Animals was conceived and written by Matt Parkins

www.ravenquest.co.uk

Thanks to my family and friends who have inspired and helped to write this book:

Sally and Laura Parkins
James Stevenson
Paul Cooper
Leo Gubert
Dave and Fran Rickwood
Jim White
Luna Burrell and the children from Okehampton Primary School
Many others who live, work and play around Dartmoor

Front cover illustrations:
Hare by Sienna Holman, Dormouse by Holly Hamel
Back cover illustrations:
Common lizard by Robbie Dalton, Kestrel by Isabella Evans

Pearl bordered fritillary by Emily Thomas

66186507R00021

Made in the USA
Charleston, SC
19 January 2017